The Loneliness Factor

With all good wishes,

Carole Oles

Bread Loaf 1990

The Loneliness Factor

Carole Oles

Carole Oles

The Loneliness Factor, by Carole Oles, is published in cooperation with the Associated Writing Programs and is a contribution to the *AWP Series for Contemporary Poetry.*

ISBN 0-89672-071-3 (paper)
ISBN 0-89672-072-1 (cloth)
Library of Congress Catalog Card Number: 78-24746
Texas Tech Press, Lubbock, Texas 79409
Copyright 1979 by Texas Tech University
Printed in the United States of America

Acknowledgments

The following poems are reprinted by permission of the publishers.

"A Catholic Girl's Confession Manual," *The Boston Phoenix*, February 11, 1975, p. 11.

"A Manifesto for the Faint-Hearted," *Poetry Northwest*, Winter 1977-1978, p. 8.

"Among Small Animals," *Seven Poets*, The Best Cellar Press, Spring 1977, pp. 26-27.

"Apple-Picking," *Prairie Schooner*, Fall 1975, p. 207.

"Brother at One Week," *Yes (A Magazine of Poetry)*, Winter 1974, p. 2.

"Coming into the United Society of Believers," *The Back Door*, Numbers 9 and 10, pp. 58-60.

"Confirmation Day," *Prairie Schooner*, Summer 1978, p. 172.

"Cycling," *Dark Horse*, Winter 1978, p. 10.

"Description of Proposed Activity," *Seven Poets*, The Best Cellar Press, Spring 1977, p. 29.

"Falling from Skyscrapers," *Poetry Northwest*, Winter 1976-1977, pp. 18-19.

"Familiars," *Prairie Schooner*, Summer 1978, pp. 170-171.

"For the Aunts," *The Poetry Miscellany*, Number 5, 1975, pp. 36-37.

"Four Parts of a Thousand-Part Poem," *Ploughshares*, Spring 1977, pp. 82-84.

"Francestown Suite," *Poetry*, November 1978, p. 82.

"From Outside the Last Room," *Quarterly West*, Winter 1978, pp. 106-107.

"Gate in Snow," *Prairie Schooner*, Summer 1978, p. 169.

"Hysterectomy in Munich," *Prairie Schooner*, Fall 1973, pp. 218-219.

"Identify What is Wrong with this Picture," *Dark Horse*, Winter 1978, p. 10.

"Making Sense in September," *Seven Poets*, The Best Cellar Press, Spring 1977, p. 28.

"Message on a Sea Wall," *The Poetry Miscellany*, Volume 8, 1978, p. 95.

"Mother and Child," *The Real Paper*, December 17, 1977, p. 52.

"Old Text," *Poetry Northwest*, Winter 1977-1978, pp. 5-6.

"One Page in *The American Heritage Dictionary*," *Poetry*, November 1978, p. 83.

"On an Airplane, Considering Night," *Poetry*, November 1978, p. 84.

"Plane Falls Apart," *Prairie Schooner*, Fall 1973, p. 219.

"Priorities," *The Beloit Poetry Journal*, Summer 1975, p. 16.

"Rain the Rememberer," *Poetry*, May 1978, p. 96.

"Remembering Rosie," *13th Moon*, Winter 1975, p. 35.

"Response to A. J. Daly," *Poetry Northwest*, Winter 1977-1978, p. 7.

"Shoes," *Prairie Schooner*, Spring 1974, p. 40.

"The Bed Poem," *The Blacksmith Anthology*, Blacksmith Press, 1976, p. 38.

"The Explanation," *13th Moon*, Winter 1975, p. 35.

"The Father-Longing," *Prairie Schooner*, Spring 1974, p. 38.

"The Gift," *13th Moon*, Number 1, 1974, p. 38.

"The Green Violinist," *Ploughshares*, Spring 1977, pp. 84-85.

"The Loneliness Factor," *Prairie Schooner*, Summer 1978, p. 168.

"The Magician Suspends the Children," *Prairie Schooner*, Fall 1975, pp. 206-207.

"The Price of Breast in Las Vegas," *New Poets: Women*, Les Femmes Press, pp. 96-97.

"The Unteaching," *Poetry Northwest*, Winter 1977-1978, p. 6.

"To Pay a Sunday Visit," *The Back Door*, Numbers 9 and 10, pp. 60-61.

"Trouble Is Interviewed on Radio," *Green House*, Winter 1978, pp. 60-61.

"Wintersong," *The Back Door*, Numbers 9 and 10, p. 62.

"Yearning for Zion," *Prairie Schooner*, Spring 1974, p. 39.

Foreword

"The best introduction to a first book of poems," the late Dudley Fitts once wrote, "is the book itself." This is particularly true in the case of Carole Oles's poems, which are lucid and compassionate. They are the product of a disciplined wit and they speak with quiet urgency to our human condition.

Fitts then went on from his opening demurrer to prologuize the Yale Series of Younger Poets winner in 1960, George Starbuck. In that same year he exercised his good offices to find a publisher for my first book. It seems especially fitting that I should now speak in behalf of a poet whose work I admire and whose formal appearance is sponsored by Texas Tech Press as part of the Associated Writing Programs *Series for Contemporary Poetry*.

In 1971 Oles turned up in my creative writing course at Newton College in Massachusetts. I was immediately struck by her technical skill with rhyme and meter and I was even more struck by the depth and resonance of her imagery. She showed then and has continued to develop an uncanny ability to convert the emotion into the poem, rather than simply exposing the nerve. I have watched her talent grow over these several years and I have taken a special pleasure in seeing this book find its shape.

In the title poem, which completes a group of poems that explore a range of man-woman relationships, Oles tells us:

> According to Einstein
> the faster you travel
> the slower time passes
> but the loneliness factor
> is constant.

She goes on to cite some chilling examples of our separation from one another—"only you warm the place/filled by your body/however close the other's face"—and ends with the image of her aging father, ill with emphysema:

> A toddler, he will soon be
> delivered. You will watch
> outside the glass, your breath
> banging, not getting through.

But the poet gets through, backward in time to childhood, as in "A Catholic Girl's Confession Manual," where she enters the box, waits for the priest to take his place and for the grill to slide back:

> Any second yours will open.
> Day like a flashlight
> will discover you.
> A drowsy human face will appear
> behind the chicken wire.
> You're on.
>
> Ready, set. Lie

In the final section of the book, a contemporary allegorical figure appears who "will be best remembered/for his work in Human Affairs." When asked to describe himself, Trouble complies:

> You'll know me anywhere.
> I am the gnat
> who slips through the screen,
> I am the middleman,
> I get between.

Metaphor, as Nemerov once defined it, mediates between a thing and a thought. Getting between is the poet's job. Carole Oles is doing just that.

Maxine Kumin
Warner, New Hampshire
July 1978

Contents

IV

V.

I

Falling from Skyscrapers

1

The first time is the hardest.
All that small movement below
and no one looking up.
X en route to the dentist,
Y to a lover Z
(yours), taxis obsessed
with their own metrics.
Don't look back
for the wringing of hands.
Expect no brass bands
at the bottom, no plaques.
Slip into air,
it has never fit better.
Dream the old dream of flight,
steer, ride your weight
down like a gull
fishing the torrent.
You will always remember
this moment.

2

Falling from skyscrapers
the second, third, so on
is like being a file clerk.
You dress for work
(sporty), put your papers
in order, act responsible.
Dream the same old dream,
of flight to the tropics
where, for you: rain.
Cast your weight down,
a stone ill-shaped
for skipping or walls.
You will try to forget these
moments, but all you know

now is falling
when what you want is to stand
on the ground
looking up, to behave
like a tree or a tourist,
like love.

Four Parts of a Thousand-Part Poem

1   Adaptation

First the fisherman's woman
asks for a double bed.
Granted.
Then one uninterrupted day
that nobody stumbles across
bearing invoices.
Granted.
Then a room apart
wherein the bed takes dominion.
Okay, okay.
Then a child to celebrate
bed, day, and room
a sailor's knot
with a blue eye and a green.
We all know where this leads.
The fisherman's woman
straining old times
through her fingers
like tea leaves.
The fisherman out dark to dark
listening just to the sea.
He has his work to do.

2   Definition

The torn lover's
good at catchy phrases,
e.g. 'My wife is my life.'
The woman tries too.
'My husband is my husband,
my life
is a gift for no occasion.
I never ordered it.
Someone paid a lot in postage.
If I move, it's forwarded.
What's inside, I put.'

3 Recreation

Hide and Seek, he says.
But she's always It.
He knows every big tree
in this forest, every cave.
He covers his tracks
like a native,
does birdcalls to stump her.
He's got all his friends
pointing This Way, the liars.
If she had time to
she'd peek, lead him
into the clearing
and explore until sundown.
How's about a little
Strip Poker? she asks.
Too scary? Is he a man,
or a story?

4 Occupation

Move over.
The border used to be there
but I've changed it.
The house with shutters
that used to be yours
is on my side.
It didn't hurt, did it?
Don't worry. You'll soon
learn my language.
The vanquished are facile.
Never mind the old country.
You'll thrive on my diet.
And even beneath a full moon,
holding the hand of the river
you won't find your way back.

Identify What Is Wrong with This Picture

A room full of moon, the old whitewash.
From the drawer, a clock ticking in spite
of the underwear trying to smother it.
Near the window a bed where the numerous man
lies with a woman whose features
he can't distinguish. Laughter
their three-legged horse, secrets their beads.
The door locked. The woman jealous of sleep.

There is no future in this picture.
These two will not need to watch years
intrude like spelling errors on the well-
developed compositions of their faces.
They will never make garbage together.
This canvas will be slashed cleanly
down the middle when morning slips
over the sill with a knife in her teeth.

The Price of Breast in Las Vegas

In the bars, the gambling rooms
all the best nightspots
silicone breasts cantilever
the drink trays, breasts
ride the footlights,
breasts are the trophy
over the doorway.
Breasts is the password.

So when he promises
'breast augmentation'
the girls leap.
Three-inch needles sink in.
His nostrils never quiver
as he pumps Johnson's Wax,
bootspray at sixty dollars a shot.
Going in, it looks like rich milk
tricked back. Coming out
is another story.
There is no small print
to tell of the pain.
.

Five years later
one woman's breasts grow golfballs,
meteors burning holes in her sleep.
Another wakes from radical
surgery with nipples pinned
under her arms.
Some permanently drop
from the chorus line,
silicone olive oil
oozing into their brains.

The survivors shower alone now.
They turn from the children.
Nightly they put out
on librium rafts
beyond the ruined orchards.

Old Text

Three things are too wonderful for me;
four I do not understand:
the way of an eagle in the sky,
the way of a serpent on a rock,
the way of a ship on the high seas,
and the way of a man with a maiden.
—Proverbs *30:18, 19*

I'll tell you.
The way of a man
with a maiden
is the way of all
three wonders.

He soars and tumbles
drawing loops in the air
which she flies into
and he cinches
pulling her down
to the pile of sticks
on the ledge.
It begins.

He's all muscle.
How can she resist?
She knows that dance.
Even the rock squirms under it.
He hardly sees her.
If she doesn't fight back
she's female.
He has no shadow
until he's erect.
Then, even the trees applaud.

Only those on the shore
call the sea Mother.
The maiden's the ship

made to dip and rise
with his moods.
He's dark-eyed
a roaring drunk
a batterer.
Remorseful in the morning.
Rolling the sun
off his tongue.

Kinds of Birds

the birds you feed
and birds that feed on you
inside your head
they steal your eyes
deface each enterprise

the birds who fly
and Big Idea birds
whose wings stay
on the ground

the park birds
hungry things no one loves
but old ladies
park birds themselves

the woods birds
startled up in yellows
against the green
the shore birds
those monochromes
chinning the horizon

the singers and clackers
divers and crack-ups
queer birds
and queer bird callers

the birds whose names you know
but will not admit to
birds who have scattered in your heart
at sunset

and the bird with the lift
of your father
in whose downdraft
you flutter

and the bird who stands on
one leg when a man and a woman
are plucked
from time's beak.

Old Couple at Howard Johnson's Soda Fountain in Manchester, New Hampshire

He steers her in like a baby carriage.
Places each jointed part
in the seat. She stays
where she's put,

all but her mouth, which neither
of them can control. Unhinged,
it stands open.
Anyone can look in.

He's attentive, smiles at her cheekbone.
She stares straight ahead,
a soldier obeying some unsaid,
inflexible orders.

He has bacon and eggs, she has a malt.
Wonderful! she picks it up,
drinks. He leans to wipe
her naughty mouth.

Try to see the girl he married
walking beside the Merrimack
wearing a picture hat, noticing. Before
the river froze.

Is this love, the kind it takes years
to make, or the Christian kind?
Or a case of not cutting off your leg
because it's asleep?

Amor vincit omnia.
Drink up and get home.

From Outside the Last Room

He Visits

She's too busy breathing to notice.
Her room faces west, gaudy now
with late sun. She drinks air
through a plastic straw, it is almost
too thick to swallow. The patient's
husband sits, consults his watch.
Nothing moves but her lungs doing pushups
and his, counting.

Her Body

He doesn't try to recall how long
since he touched her that way.
As if she'd betrayed him, he couldn't
compete. He gathers her fingers,
those twigs, that kindling. She's
growing backwards into the small
bones of newborns, the baldness.
He's a scientist. There is no God.
He plans each lecture twice, rakes leaves,
jogs further, drinks bourbon. Finally
sleeps.

The Loom

The Swedish oak's more than sturdy enough.
North light falls on the half-realized
pattern. The wool cost too much,
she admitted. It was made to last.
Now he wants to kick the legs off the frame,
burn it, slice through the threads.
He resists, shuts the door. Nothing
can stop it.

The Friends

Amen. One stone replaces another.
Their talk cuts figure 8's, they keep him
volleying, distract him with their sons.
He should travel. There are so many
lonely women. He's always welcome
to dinner.

What Will

Spring will send in its front guard
of crocuses, forsythia will follow
with banners, rain will loosen the earth
for the small mouths of tulips, birds
will bring morning in on the red
carpets of their throats, and he will. He
will, he will.

The Loneliness Factor

According to Einstein
the faster you travel
the slower time passes
but the loneliness factor
is constant. For example

nothing smiles for the camera on Mars
but Olympus Mons 15 miles high
and they say that stars
including our own
fling outward from the Milky Way.

Here on Earth
on November-cold bedsheets
only you warm the place
filled by your body
however close the other's face.
Always news arrives
in an envelope marked Private,
always you stand at the gate
with your hand in your hand.

And, for example
your father contracts, shuttles
between TV and the kitchen.
He travels nowhere slowly
on rationed air. Glue
licks his lungs.
A toddler, he will soon be
delivered. You will watch
outside the glass, your breath
banging, not getting through.

II

To Pay a Sunday Visit

Don't forget chalk
to keep your maryjanes white.
Follow your mother and father
up four flights through
the layered smell of hallways:
underwear, sweat, something
stewing, and behind it all
the exterminator's talcum.

Kiss the pleats on Aunt Sadie's
cheek. Tell her you've
missed her, you're in second
grade now. Say hello
to dear Gertrude who tats
in the corner. Sit still
and don't suck your braids.

In the front room don't ask
about the cartons. So what
if they're crowding
the ceiling. Don't wave
to strangers brushing by
on the 3rd Avenue El.
And hands off the piano.

If Gert serves you
milk with a baby roach
paddling toward shore,
lock yourself in the bathroom.
If you meet the big ones
in there, don't yell for
your mother. At rush hour
on the woodwork, they
know who's boss.

Don't shuffle your feet
at the door. When the last

goodbye sputters, walk
don't run to the street.
Lie back in the Chevy.
Say please when you
ask for some air.
Watch through the windshield.
Sunday's flushing away
and you're clean.

Mother and Child

No I said, and stood.
It was summer.
You were tired and hot
on Steinway Street,
your feet swollen.
Your eighth month
floating the boy
who would die.

No I screamed
and ladies passing
tut-tutted.
When I looked around
you were gone.
I was marooned,
thirsty among the tall people,
my hands full of August.

Years later you told
how you'd hidden in a doorway
watching fear
turn me supple.
You rushed over
when enough was enough.

Mother,
I am out in this street
with no hat on.
The pavement shimmers
and writhes, lovers pass
with their smiles in their pockets.
Mother, be in the doorway
ready to rain.

Brother at One Week

Brother's cradle
doesn't rock
to lullabies
Mother doesn't hum.

So perfect in the box,
he is too perfect.
Maiden aunts
dab monogrammed hankies:
It's all for the best.

Mother's sails
hang slack
in the calm,
her smile capsizes.
Seaweed
and sandy blue beds
are on her mind.

Tomorrow Mother
will curl her hands
into trowels.
She will rake the earth
with her teeth
to carve out a hole,
a quite small burrow.
Tucking him in,
with mother-gut
she will sew up
the gash.

The Explanation

I am pushed backwards
into the sea at 12,
ears stinging
with jellyfish.

Mother's face near me
hides in the room
where her whisper
stubs against my bed.

My lot, she explains,
to bleed in darkness:
sit in Latin class
bleeding
next to Arthur Schublin;

jump rope
running blood
on the pavement,
the rope
struck to red;

eat meals
with Father,
the hot secret
between my legs
and him knowing it.

"Nothing
to be ashamed of,"
she says. "Growing up."
Show me your face, Mother.

She turns away
to lighted rooms.
I fall through unlit
waters toward
the coral beds below.

Remembering Rosie

who died at 30

Rosie. I see us swinging in the cage
of strapless gowns, you with
the college freshman from New Jersey,
me with the red-cheeked boy
who turns up one day in drag on 42nd Street.
Afflicted, you pin spare Kotex
like a Purple Heart inside your hem.

At Lake Ronkonkoma we balance
our 2-wheelers into summer evenings
stuffy with canasta, onion cookies.
There's your mother telling childbirth
stories, your brother strangled
in the liferope, you wrenched
awake that night in knots.

We plant victory gardens, long for
uncles at the front, shell bracelets
from the Philippines. Outside Room 202
winter's dotted swiss falls.
Deep in our clothes, we brave
the blizzard stout as tanks.
That other war goes on.
But us, we make it home
past Harry Dracon's iceballs.

Remember how we dress grownup
to visit Mother at the Lying-In
the year my sister's born?
To get upstairs we have to be 13.
If only we can keep these hats straight
and stop laughing, we can be old.

We march to Elgar
wars before renewal takes P.S.5.
Without the slightest effort
we begin to gray.
The child you didn't have
jams in the adding machine.
You're at home in a geography
we didn't learn. Rosie, Rosie,
the enemy went indoors.

For the Aunts

When their bones have been ground
into talcum and we stand in the rain,
not warmed even by the huddle
of our related bodies, making light
of the aunts will be out of the question.
None of us will be tempted to laugh

as I'm told Viola had to laugh
so hard she slipped on icy ground
to see me newborn—without question
the reddest, mangiest joke to rain
down on the family since light
first drew it from the cave-huddle.

Viola, that starched girl, would huddle
at her window while a young man's laugh
climbed to her from beneath the porch light.
Despite the father he stood his ground,
sent her promises fierce as summer rain.
She breathed faster waiting for the question.

In Viola's day no good girl dared to question
a father's judgment. No democratic huddle
would decide her fate. Papa, Suzerain
delivered his decrees and never learned to laugh.
In his parlor young men's hopes ran aground
and Viola wore darkglasses in the moonlight.

As for Edwina, the sister with a voice light
as petals falling, she asked a dreadful question:
to debark for Europe, study opera—grounds
for disowning daughters. "*My* Edwina, in a huddle
of swarthy men who scarcely even laugh
in English? Never!" Her tears outdid the rain,

but Edwina stayed home too, on fatherly terrain.
She learned to be a seamstress, did light
housekeeping. People say she'll often laugh
while turning a French seam, or answer questions
no one hears. In corners of her mind arias huddle
as she dart-throws common pins into the ground.

In the cold rain where we huddle and laugh
too loud when light is gone, even the ground
shakes; even stones turn and question.

The Father-Longing

A tapeworm inhabits us.
No number of fingers, legs,
tongues can satisfy.
Each day we run
to an empty mailbox;
each day like widows
we scan the horizon.
Our hearts are new moons,
our lips broken records
playing the same
old word.

You might never guess.
We drive standard-shift cars
earn Bachelor's Degrees
ride elevators
marry.
But a question mark
hangs in the closet
and hooks in the throat.

O Daddy, why,
why didn't you lie
me those three little words?

Where the hook goes in
the self leaks silently
out.

The Bed Poem

Your name for his,
Father. It's legal, right
that we lie here together,
a perfect jigsaw
of notches and bulges.
Twice I have swallowed
his magic fish,
hiccuped it back into air
wearing ears
and somebody's nose.
Stay out of it, Father
on the other side of the wall,
your stale cigar smoke
a spy at the keyhole.
I'm not 15 and surprised
in the back seat of a Chevy.
I'm not kicking too high
or bending too low.
I've only learned
what you never would tell,
you with the babe on your keyring,
you with the glossy nudes
in your handkerchief drawer.
You go to sleep now.
Stop listening. It's over
between us. I go home with him.

The Gift

Thinking she was the gift
they began to package it early.
They waxed its smile
they lowered its eyes
they tuned its ears to the telephone
they curled its hair
they straightened its teeth
they taught it to bury its wishbone
they poured honey down its throat
they made it say yes yes and yes
they sat on its thumbs.

That box has my name on it,
said the man. *It's for me.*
And they were not surprised.

While they blew kisses and winked
he took it home. He put it on a table
where his friends could examine it
saying *dance* saying *faster.*
He plunged its tunnels
he burned his name deeper.
Later he put it on a platform
under the lights
saying *push* saying *harder*
saying *just what I wanted*
you've given me a son.

Hysterectomy in Munich

They pry her mouth open.
My sister is gassed.
This operation has been done before.
Records will be properly kept.
While she flies a Klieg light
over a peagreen sea
the surgeon gives orders.
A stainless West German
knife sinks in her belly.
Blood grows
like time-lapsed poppies.

Across the city
twin phalluses
of Frauenkirche
maintain their erections
as for five centuries.
At Nuremberg Stadium
her friends cheer
a rock group.
The surgeon paints
sterile cotton
bright carnelian.
He is a hummingbird
x-ing his needlepoint.
Tissue drops into
plastic bags.
She rides a slab
to the recovery room

where she climbs back
with lead bells chained
to both ankles
with staples punched
in her tear.
Over her head

a Bavarian moon
opens its mouth.
Two Bavarian dumplings
sway above her
and though she is free,
white, and twenty
she cries for the room
for the language
for the mother
she has cut away.

Cycling

Julie, when I see you
close your eyes
and coast down the
hill at top speed

I see you with him
your mouth taking the air
like a funnel
as you pedal in tandem
up up up
up and over

I see you pump out a baby
take that corner
leaning in
swallowing salt

Even at five
you want breasts
want a furry place
and holes in your ears

I see you ride past my house
get small
make your own tracks
into the dangerous traffic

III

A Catholic Girl's Confession Manual

Dress up for God.

Walk past the rectory
so Fr. Brophy sees you
going to confess.
Say, "Good afternoon,
Fr. Brophy," in your
most upsucking voice.

Before entering church
cover your magnificent
hair with a scarf
so as not to arouse
the Lord's passion.

Be not aroused by candles, vaults, or incense.

Get in the shortest line.
Hope it's your favorite
priest—the one who laughs.

Run through it:
recall how you watched
the little boy pee
at the curb outside
Quinn's Funeral Home.
Feel guilty.

Wait your turn patiently.
Don't notice how long
the priest holds
the one before you.
When he finally exits,
consider your shoes.

Pull back the velvet
curtain and enter. The box

will be crowded with darkness.
Don't panic. Right face.
Kneel.

Try to get what the one
on the other side is saying.
Breathe deeply when you
hear his window shut.

Any second yours will open.
Day like a flashlight
will discover you.
A drowsy human face will appear
behind the chicken wire.
You're on.

Ready, set. Lie.

The Arm of St. Francis

Something is special.
Soon it will be bedtime but
I am wearing my navy blue coat
riding the BMT with Mother.

Above ground, night nibbles
my ears and climbs my bare legs.
We stand in the line
that circles the Church
of Our Lady of the Assumption.

I am pushed through the doorway
into a country of elbows.
I can move without walking,
without knowing where
or whose hand I am holding.

It takes longer than History
to get where the people stop.
Now I am sweaty and tired
of breathing wool. Mother leans
to whisper *At the altar
we'll kiss the glass case.*

Hot things crawl on my head,
my stomach turns cartwheels.
God! don't make me do it—
I will never lie again,
never fight Doris Bilik.

I am pulled to my knees
and the priest with the case
is sidestepping this way.
I can't look, I will cry
or have an accident,

I try to close my eyes in time
but I have already seen
when I bend to kiss the glass
over the bone of the man
who is dead and

missing this bone from his arm
this bone on red velvet
like expensive jewelry,
like the key to a city.

Confirmation Day

Your head goes AWOL
at the Church of His Most Precious Blood.
Black water knocks down your doors.
They carry you out.

You wake where sun is off-limits
in a house of ignorance: no books allowed.
You blemish the sheets,
a rage of poppies.

Get up!—the Bishop is waiting.
Red ants storm the walls of your mouth.
Help is a fish gliding onto your forehead,
your lids flutter like white flags.

This is measles at 12,
the beginning of knowledge.
You sailing out like a ghost ship
and God in his kitchen
carving the lamb.

Yearning for Zion

I have always wanted to be one.
Some of my best friends are.
I have wanted to wear the special
star, speak the deep language, be free
of the son and his ghostly rewards.

O mystery of matzoh, fabulous gefilte fish!
All my god ever gave me were gummed labels
to swallow and a bone almost clean
under my pillow. Long ago, Thelma Roseman
and I swapped shoes for a day.
I tried to keep hers for that long
walk to temple. Thelma, I prayed, let me in
to the Friday night candles and blessings,
no priest in place but your father.
Let me in to the empty pockets of your Saturdays.
Let me wash with the unscented soap
that asks no apologies. Let us remember together
uncles and cousins smudged on the Polish sky.

Once I nearly squeezed in through the crack
of marriage but couldn't quite fit. Still,
years later giving birth to a son
the miraculous word on my lips was
oi.
O Daughters of Zion, lift me in your hennaed hands;
Abraham, let me lie in your bosom.
I have always wanted to be there.
Some of my only friends are.

Seeing the Ruins

Pyramid, Chichen Itza, Yucatan

It means to tell us we're little.
Even with our longer legs
we're beetles scaling a wall.
We stop counting steps,
lose the idea of future.
We're hauling one limb at a time.

When we reach the top, it's Mother,
Home. But we see we've swum
out too far, with no craft
to get us back. Climbing, we had stones
to lean on. Going down, we'll be adrift
in space. Did they think this, the ones
who returned? Or were crops,
the gods' gladness, enemies, foremost

in their minds as they stepped
over the edge? Did the high priest
waver, pressing the knife on the young
belly? How thin the cries must have sounded
here above the trees. At this angle,
how quickly life would flow down.

We traverse like novices,
zig by zag to the ground.
In the road two men laugh, playing catch.
We look closer. The ball's dead: a bird.

Coming into the United Society of Believers

Shaker Village Restoration and Museum,
Hancock, Massachusetts.

Even the dancing is 'Labouring,'
meaning either labor is pleasure
or only dressed up as labor
does pleasure get into this village.
In the Sisters' House a girl
named Cathy minuets with the wool,
two turns of the wheel, a step back
then forward and turn again,
thock as it fattens the spool.

The men are thin-lipped.
They save themselves
for seeding the fields.
All the while a whole city
with towers and rivers and hammering clocks
forms on the mist of their breath,
settles in drops on their eyelids.
Down the hall the women
sleep in shallows, dream
blazing trees
    " 'The Tree of Light or Blazing Tree'
    seen and received by Hannah Cohoon"
they indent the tight beds
with their tossing to
and away from
that terrible fire.

And the ice. They haul it three-fourths
of a mile to the Ice House
the giant's toolbox
with tongs for his splinters
picks for his pullman-car teeth
and the pack of yapping saws.
The brethren sent ice square and true
swaddled in shavings down

the Housatonic, down the Charles,
down the Amazon.
O true Americans! Wily virgins. Believers
in commerce.

In the round stone barn
a ring dance of
104 velvet cows' eyes.
The diplomats ruminate, wait
for the call to circle left.
All spokes on the great wheel,
they drop platters of praise
the fields' nugget.
This holy house soars
to the clerestory,
the Christ-eye looking in.

'This saw is still capable
of cutting wood,' the sign says.
Spinning wheel, swift,
and squirrel cage are capable.
The orchard still delivers
to The Good Room,
the herb garden yields
Feverfew, Hardhack,
Bugle Bitter, Life Everlasting.
The bonnets, capes,
boots are still.

Brethren and sisters
have entered their bone season.
They bundle now,
they who would not
pass each other on stairs.

Francestown Suite

for Jabez Holmes, d. May 11, 1824,
Francestown, New Hampshire

Nice place you have here, Jabez Holmes.
At the center of town but still quiet.
Don't bother, I'll sit on this stone
turtle's back. Moss breaks through the granite
but nothing I do can interrupt your work.
Where is everyone else? We're alone.
Does Francestown liven up after dark?
All I hear is a power saw's moan
at the throat of a pine. The tree holds
its tongue. On the dead air, suddenly a smell
a vital sign rises: manure. The gelded
Morgan tests his barbed wire wall.
And look, Jabez. Empty bottles of Tuborg.
Now, running, two kids with a red dog.

                               °

It must have been hard here. I mean more
than the granite. I mean cold and hungry hard
waiting and praying hard, nothing for the fevers.
Jabez, for instance, with two wives in this sod
before him and thirty years to live out alone.
His Sally, only daughter, stopped at three.
There must have been times when Jabez ran
out of faith and drank too much brandy
or whipped the horses. Times when a watered silk
gown made Sarah, Elizabeth dance in his mind
again. Anniversaries he'd rather not think
about, hand-knitted mufflers he wouldn't find.
Days when Jabez wondered what for
and walked miles over fresh snow, anywhere.

                               °

The clock tower of the Old Meeting House,
gathered 1773, sends four
clear notes to the ruffled sky. Loss
is what I am thinking of. How the shore
recedes, how the headstones these boats
toss in time's groundswell and the names
wear thin. I see Sarah who ballasts the oak
floating out in the 36th year of her age,
Jabez turning his face into the wind.
Eight years later, Elizabeth at 37.
Here, I am old enough to be underground
too, incognito. So are my children.
We did it, you can, sings the chorus.
On 136 West, the logging trucks pass.

Message on a Sea Wall

Where the wall says stop
he climbs down.
The ocean steps back.
It's winter, and henna trees gape.
He works while the town fathers sleep.

Others have been here. Paul,
writing 'Heather, I love ya,'
Doug and Brenda, Norman and Syl.
But he's different,
had asthma, was always too small.

Starting over his head,
slowly he sprays words down the rough
stones, sinks to his knees.
The letters will come up each day.
Beachcombers, commuters will find

JESUS IS STILL THE ANSWER.

But what was the question?
How to, in the dark night?
Where, in the city of flame?
Jesus is still the answer

after Heather and Paul
go out on the heart's tide,
after the shore counts its wrecks,
and the moon walks him home.

Familiars

1

Spider sanctifies the writing table
floats above it on inverted guy wires
rows upper air with eight paddles
now she bobs like a yoyo now hovers
as thought rushes in upside-down.
From her gut she is spinning the
story of thread. Come spider, teach.

2

Fly, show yourself!
for I am inflamed
with a righteous wrath
I strike out
with my paper sword.
You buzz my tower
touch-and-go.
You engine of nightmares
you rumor
you forecast.
Scram.
Sell yourself to a dead cod.
Drink a cesspool.

3

Darning-needle
knows how to sit still
and when.
Self-assured in the sun
she lets me come close
to find the trick wings.
They pulse at the throat of the air
she is what you call
keeping her options open.
I stare at her eyes
and the yellow mask underneath.
Sister! I think. Healer.

The Magician Suspends the Children

With this charm I keep the boy at six
and the girl fast at five
almost safe behind the four
walls of family. We three
are a feathery totem I tattoo
against time: I'll be one

again. Joy here is hard-won
but possible. Protector of six
found toads, son, you feel too
much, my Halloween mouse. Your five
finger exercises predict no three
quarter time gliding for

you. Symphonic storms are the fore-
cast, nothing unruffled for my wun-
derkind. Have two children: make three
journeys upstream. Son, at six
you run into angles where five
let you curve, let me hold onto

your fingers in drugstores. Too
intent on *them*, you're before
or behind me five
paces at least. Let no one
tie the sturdy boat of your six
years to me the grotesque, the three

headed mother. More than three
times you'll deny me. And my cockatoo,
my crested girl, how you cry to be six.
Age gathers on your fore-
head with that striving. Everyone
draws your lines and five

breaks out like a rash, five
crouches, pariah of the three
o'clock male rendezvous. Oh won-
derful girl, my impromptu
rainbow, believe it: you'll be four-
teen before you're six.

This is the one abracadabra I know to
keep us three, keep you five and six.
Grow now. Sing. Fly. Do what you're here for.

Plane Falls Apart

The paper shows a man
facedown in his seat
his only foot wearing no shoe.
I try to keep my mind
from turning him over.
The TV says the sole survivor
exceeded human tolerances.
His chances are poor.
I hide the paper
from the children
hide the children
from the TV.

What was I doing?
Smoking? Talking on the phone?
No cocks crowed at noon.
The ferns didn't shrivel.
The cat didn't lose her appetite.

What can I do?
Write a letter to the paper
to the airline, to the airport?
Write a letter to God
telling him he can't do this
telling him there are laws?

hide the paper
hide the children

Description of Proposed Activity

With luck I'll open my eyes.
Find him beside me.
With luck he'll be breathing,
stoking his dreams.

I'll hear the weather report
on the leaves, see what's
new in the way light
fingers the ceiling.

My bladder will ring
like a fire alarm,
my feet will say flat
goodmornings to the floor.

I'll wave my hand
and orange juice fountains
will leap, an incense
of coffee will bless the air.

I'll climb into the cloth
of the day, flatten
my spare and zip up,
thinking *Please fit.*

IV

Among Small Animals: A Riddle Poem

1

If his luck holds
he may crawl through
two hundred winters.
He goes on four plates,
wears a cup on his back.
He retreats to that dome
as old men take rooms
in their memories.

2

It's these who last.
We all keep a tryst
with them. They grow
on us; together we endow
the field. Spineless as noodles,
they drown up in puddles.
Halved, they survive.

3

Their admirers form a society.
Some write poems to these
libertines, wearers of silk.
These walk on cushions,
see by slit lanterns,
claw open our nights
when they cry out for mates.

4

None so quiet as this one:
she hears all, never tells.
Her nose is a jittery lappet,
her foot works magic.
Sword-swallower of greens,
promiscuous breeder, she lives short;
runs, for the most part.

5

Ourselves and not.
Most valued by those without.
We walk through fire for them,
they give us back ashes.
So they undo the ties, swim
away from our beaches.
We want their days clear,
want them to sit in themselves
as in easy chairs,
want mouths telling them
yes, yes. Good.

Apple-Picking

The trees are falling
down the hillside
down into the valley
of the town of Stow
falling with the
weight of apples

the branches sag
with red balls
it is Christmas
and Isaac Newton
walks among us
as we walk amazed
among the apples

apples tempting
apples throwing themselves
at our feet, apples diving
into our mouths, apples

apples, today is
the birthday of the apple
and we are glad to be
here you and I
and our 2 native golden
delicious, their cheeks bulging,
chins dripping, mouths pressing
sweet juice from this earth
this planet Apple.

Response to A. J. Daly,
Specialist in 'Permanizing,'
Postmarked Provincetown

Dear Mr. Daly, Thanks
for your offer to 'permanize'
this clipping about me.
But I'm writing to tell you
about noon on the beach.
The bodies. From the splayed
legs and surrendered feet,
you can tell they're goners.
No blood, but poisonous quiet
under the sun's drumming.
Even the sea's tongue cut out,
no water until the Point,
a period on the horizon.

Over the flats, more bodies.
Crabs belly-up, squid with ten
useless arms, flies drinking
their eyes. And mill-ends:
the lower jaw of a bluefish
biting on air, scales dried
to fingernails, bones too small
to extrapolate from. And shells,
whole city blocks of rooms
where no one makes love.

Mr. Daly, for a dollar-fifty
with your sparkling clear
plastic and special equipment
can you protect me forever
against moisture, soiling
and the wear due to handling?
Mr. Daly, at night here
the foghorn persists in its
two wornout notes, question
and answer. The sea, that reformer,
works its dark industry. Free.

One Page in *The American Heritage Dictionary*

Debridement is the word you want to check
having read last night how Nancy Sokol
in 3rd year of medical school at Bellevue
does it for Mr. McGowan, once strapping,
now lashed to the bedpost, gnashing
his teeth, sweating profusely. 'The surgical
excision of dead and devitalized tissue'
bluntly, cutting away on his 12-inch-square
bedsore. There is nothing debonair
about him. Life is the death-trap
he's caught in. No Deborah to lead him out
nor DeBakey to furnish a cure. He stares
at the death's head moth, loses the debate,
so will Simone DeBeauvoir.
He couldn't care less about presidents,
political parties. Socialism won't share
this. The debit side's too long for a rally.
He will not tour Debrecen in Hungary.
Debilitated, he couldn't walk if they
let him. Tall Mr. McGowan is becoming debris.

Recluse

The phone smelled of her breath
so she wouldn't go near it.

Her hands looked like shovels
so she left them in a snowbank.

Her mouth was a door.
She locked it.

Her eyes were insubordinate.
She fired them.

The mirror threw a party
and she didn't know anyone.

The windows hid.
They had all the blankets.

Only the cats understood
her fish-stare.

They prowled her mind like seasons,
she went out in them.

They were the only streets
she would cross.

She lived with old news
and made headlines.

When they found her
she was dressed to kill.

At Boston Public Library

In the Humanities Room
the windows are barred
but it's warm and dry
and the books don't edge away.

Never mind if cheap wine
is a flower that
breathes from lapels
and broken zippers are smiles.

So what if this woman
who finds a lost son
stuck in the copier
sings him a lullaby

if the captain's raincoat
is three inches short everywhere
and he fell into sludge
and forgot to wash after

if the one in the coonskin cap
has misplaced his socks
the one in the wheelchair
snores at the fiction.

The librarian's busy.
Overhead the fluorescents
say *hmmm* while defeat
compiles its anthologies.

The Unteaching

A social worker was sent into the 3rd grade class that had witnessed its teacher shot and killed by her estranged husband. She was sent to assure the class that school is a safe place.

—UPI

She talks about the law
of averages. How many storms it would take
before lightning struck one of them.
How often they would have to fly.
As she speaks, they glance at the door
he came in by, they trace
the stain on the hardwood floor.

She does not mention the law of opposites,
love and hate for example. How they cohabit.
Or the law of gravity, demonstrated
by the teacher's falling. Or the law of
conservation of matter: that nothing is lost,
the teacher lives in another form.

She talks about sick people,
says they need help.
A girl with braids is yawning—
she has slept fitfully—a red-headed boy
sits rigid, as if he hears her through water.
His study habits will not improve.

The children are not stupid.
As she talks on and on
they do not relinquish the one priceless
picture of their teacher crumbling
before a blackboard spattered with lessons.

The Green Violinist

a painting by Marc Chagall

Bigger than houses, than in fact
the whole village including the church
which falls out the bottom,
he's in space, a purple motley
against pale ground. He's a 3-legged
stool, with the aid of a chimney.
High, he plays himself sick, or well.
The green advances or retreats,
face and bow hand have it.

A dog looks up, paws on a rooftop.
Someone planned to pick apples, left
the ladder against the tree which he found
bare, except for the large bird.
Or maybe the bird climbed the ladder.

A small violinist threatens the green man.
If he could reach, he'd splinter that head
with his minor violin. Where clouds
invade the horizon, a villager hitches
his wagon, will ride out of the picture.

By the house, someone has just lost
(like a child's balloon) the man who rides
clouds, who's more bird than the one
in the tree. The green man plays on
though his mustache hangs crooked,
nose bends, eyes open too wide.

This is a study in letting go.
The green violinist has put from him
the village, the rival,
the tree has surrendered its leaves,
the man in the sky has given up weight,
the dog smiles goodbye to the master.
Even as notes fly away
the green violinist, who knows,
grins and releases the bow.

A Manifesto for the Faint-Hearted

Don't curse your hands,
the tangle of lines
there. Look how
in the deepening snow
your feet make blue fish
no one can catch.

Don't take personally
the defection of leaves.
You can't be abandoned
by what you never owned.
Spring will give back more
green than you can bear.

Don't rest by the hearth
when all you're worth
tells you *Run!*
If the fires within
strangle, not even suns
will comfort your bones.

You're not so special.
The jungle's full of animals
whose guts invert
when a stronger one parts
the camouflage, peers through
as they climb a tree.

Don't think you're different.
The world's full of runts,
stutterers like yourself
who'd save all they have
not to lose it.
They lose it.

Leave trails, be separate,
dress warm, travel light.
Eat fear to grow muscle,
even Olympic champs fall.
Store advice
in a cool, dry place.

Gate in Snow

The gate lies down in snow.
Craters beside it
where 2 pairs of boots sank in deep.

Against the banked sky, crows
cut themselves out.
Squirrels dare the space between trees.

I can't tell with authority how
they perform such feats
or why, or even tell who's

said goodbye to whom in this snow,
this splintered light.
The world is full of surprises

the way I remember you now
walking through the airport gate,
becoming abstract on TWA

and remember the sparrow,
gift from a neighbor's cat—
so heavy, so unflightworthy.

V

Trouble Bathes on Such Days

when the sky is a frown
the sky with its bushy eyebrows
the sky is a gunrunner

when the air is a pendant
made of base metal
the air means to burst

jolt the complacent leaves
and outshout the trees' orations
the air is packed as Verdun

on such days
Trouble stands in the open
innocent, hairless as Buddha

Trouble hates to be kept waiting
he wants to see the lightning
and bathe in the soft waters

Trouble hates to be sweaty

Trouble Is Interviewed on Radio

Tell us about your early, formative years.

A man and woman had me.
Immigrants from Eastern Europe.
As a child, I loved fires,
never got caught.
The school said Dependable:
perfect attendance.
I ate all my supper
and drank all my milk.
When I kicked the cat
she felt the guilt.

What made you decide to specialize?

The worldwide need,
a natural bent.
I don't mind the long hours.
I love to invent.

But how does a bad press make you *feel?*

I feel with my hands
I stand on my feet
I keep my nose clean
I keep my eyes peeled
I keep my ears cocked
I keep my mouth shut
I hold my tongue
I hold an election
I win.

For our listeners, would you describe your appearance?

Some call me short,
some call me tall.
I'm more dark than fair.
I smile broadly,
my jaw is set.
You'll know me anywhere.
I am the gnat
who slips through the screen,
I am the middleman.
I get between.

Trouble's Obituary Appears

Trouble, internationally prominent,
would have been eternal on Tuesday.

Trouble earned his Ph.D. from Harvard
in 1939. His marriages ended in divorce
but they stayed the best of friends.

Trouble was a Fellow of the Institute.
Trouble served in government, industry,
and consulted in the arts.

Trouble will be best remembered
for his work in Human Affairs.

Trouble left his eyes to science.
Trouble's ashes will be scattered
from the Eastern Air-Shuttle
between New York and Washington.

Trouble is survived.
At this writing
the *Times* could not determine
how many are his children.

Making Sense in September

Saturday night again.
The children curled around
their warm breath.
Outside the leaves brazen
for a last fling.
You at repair work
a bathroom light globe
to replace the one I broke
in a fury of mopping
after leaving and coming back.
Me patching your pants
making sense
making do
against good advice
cutting my teeth on the thread.

Frost

We rescue what we can.
Tomatoes, puny red army,
make their stand
on the sill. Green squash weigh
in on the counter. But word
of the oak leaves must be passed
sotto voce: coughing up blood
again, won't last.
Even the pines show fatigue,
tobacco-stained whiskers.

As for you and me, no plague
or peril this October.
We fall more slowly
but no less down.
Warm, near sleep, you hold me.
We rescue what we can.

Wintersong

March. All day the sky sloughs off,
up for a new skin, a better or brighter fit.
Polka-dotting the air, huffing, snow
might stand still and we move. But
I am tonight in the same place,

the winter weevil has chewed a little deeper
this time, rusted my chances to get What I Want
or even to know it if it falls from the sky
like flakes or pertinent blackbirds;

I've closed off rooms too expensive to heat,
walked the chill corridors back to forget
where they locate themselves, hidden
them except from dreams, those private eyes.

If a face arranges itself in the tumble of snow
saying every goodbye, it is only snow
and silent. The elm's scrawny fingers will fatten,
earth's put-on will green.

Priorities

Forget the rest.
It's the teeth that count,
surer than thumbs
or strawberry birthmarks.
Value what lasts;
let go what easily burns.

At first there are none.
Then the bulbs push up,
punctual as desire.
Their second chances
allow for the eating of words.

Forget the flesh,
that Mae West, that old falsie.
Nourish the teeth.
Let them go down full-house,
a necklace of smiles.

Shoes

They wait for the right occasion
tapping their toes in closets.
True husbands and wives,
sundered they die.
They can be teachers,
make heels introspect
or whole bodies give up
the delusion of balance.
Runners, dancers, nurses, and fullbacks
take purpose from them.
They have never informed
the feet of newborns.

Tongues that tell no news
slings holding no rocks
platforms no campaigners debate:
we are running you, walking you,
dancing you down
to the day of last shoes—
the ones we won't know we're wearing
the ones that can't wait.

On an Airplane, Considering Night

Light holds in the stratosphere.
Night doesn't fall,
dark starts down there.

All day it piles up like bills
in the towers and houses,
in the cigarette butts
of officials and in blouses
of women who wait.

Dark collects in the children's ears,
fills the mouths of old men
who almost. Dark wears
the grass. Birds listen
and when dark says *now*
they sing *no comment.*

Like a sigh from below
night lifts through the air vent,
like a widow
night reaches to touch what it can't.

Rain the Rememberer

Rain retells every sad story
you thought you could bury

in some Potter's Field
or Pacific of the mind.

Rain brings the family
together to claim the body,

there are more relatives
than anyone needs to have.

Rain brings the red-headed boy
who is still sailing away

and the roustabout boy crushed
by the oil rig his folks wished

would make a man of him,
and the longed-for baby who came

with a hole in her heart,
a big enough door for her exit

and the ex-beauty who bore
her typewriter through 50 years

of service, outliving brothers, alone
in the large house she can't clean

and the lovers everywhere apart
waiting their only lives out,

rain not willing to forget.

Driving at Midnight, in Rain

This is the break-in hour.
Trees tote their shadows,
hedges lean their dense
secrets into the houses
while sleepers disarm.

On Beacon Street, blue lights
flash from cruisers,
a man reaches
to hold up the rain.

This is the breakdown hour.
The unsleepers pace
where no moons rise.
Hedges jabber,
leaves flap like injuries.

The dog who floats down night
in the ark of his ribs
overturns barrels.
Under the streetlight's corona,
a pile of scrapings and bones.

This is the break-up hour.
On the island of their bed, she
lies stiffly to the west,
he coughs at the silence.
They both pretend sleep

as if none of it matters.
In the dark the set of their jaws,
the hard lines of denial are hidden.
Rain makes the lies grow.

I grip the wheel tightly
as if I could control this
hour of ruptures, heart's midnight
when fear breaks the surface
and leaves me holding my breath.